Talking Razzmatazz

Talking Razzmatazz

Poems by Judy Ruiz

University of Missouri Press
Columbia and London

Library of Congress Cataloging-in-Publication Data

Ruiz, Judy.
  Talking razzmatazz : poems / by Judy Ruiz.
    p.   cm.
  ISBN 0-8262-0771-5. — ISBN 0-8262-0772-3 (pbk.)
  I. Title.
PS3568.U395T35   1991
811'.54—dc20   90-20175
                                                 CIP

The author is grateful to the editors of the publications in which the following
poems first appeared: "Aunt Macy's Dream," "Big Dipper," and "Idaho Wood,"
in *Rectangle*; "Basic Witch Poem," in *Piedmont Literary Review*; "Explain," "I Give
Me That," and "Speech," in *Rocky Mountain Writers Forum*; "A Fantasy Death
Has Just Before Dawn," in *New Mexico Humanities Review*; "Golden" and "Small
Play Called Get the Beat," in *River City Review*; "The Lemons" and "Maybe
Someday" in *Midwest Quarterly*; "Nirvana or What Happens When You Think
God Looks Just Like You," in *Quarterly* (as "Nirvana"); "Saint Peter to the Boring
Poet," "The Vessel," and "Windhorses," in *Along the River*; "Send Me a Soldier,"
in *Peace or Perish: A Crisis Anthology*; "While Making a Pencil Sketch of Eggs with
the Sun So Perfectly Burning," in *Primavera*.

Designer: Rhonda Gibson
Typesetter: Connell-Zeko Type & Graphics
Printer: Thomson-Shore, Inc.
Binder: Thomson-Shore, Inc.
Typeface: Usherwood Bold Italic and Palatino

Contents

Talking Razzmatazz

Basic Witch Poem

In daylight, find her bent in heart
talking to small rabbits who have no heads
and do not care to have them.

In daylight, find her sighing
through the playgrounded children of America
with no fear of rain or recess bells.

In daylight, find her smartly dressed
and sitting perfectly next to you on a bus
going to Idaho. Notice she has an orange for a suitcase.

Of course she does this well. After all,
we're dealing with a woman who eats
small baskets for breakfast.

Of course she has no shame. After all,
we're dealing with a woman who never
sorts her laundry right and always wins at cards.

And of course she's beautiful. After all,
we're dealing with a woman
who at the first cry of witch
begins to gather her own wood
and who's always had *her* way with fire.

Idaho Wood

It's near the end of January
when I notice I'm not poetic anymore
and maybe never have been, except once
when a publisher paid me seventy dollars
for some lines about a witch who gathered
her own wood after a bus ride to Idaho.

I could have had her grope for Idaho
potatoes, but no, I gave her an orange in January
and set her out in the real world gathering
sticks, being beautiful, wanting no more
than what the absence of a million dollars
could buy in an open market once—

once upon a time, when words like once
meant something big had happened. Before Idaho,
she cast spells on people who had dollars,
went south to Sante Fe in January,
broke bread with the Indians, and had more
God than any pentecostal gathering.

I made her have a way with fire, out there, gathering
her wood in empty prairies like the cosmic peasant who
    once
had a flare for the hearth, but then said, "No more.
You're not leaving me out here in the middle of Idaho

in this damn dark at the crummy end of January
with nothing in terms of sense and dollars."

I was the poet. I knew no one would give her any dollars.
I knew the lack of berries would make gathering
difficult, and I knew how harsh January
could be even in the furriest of boots. See, once
I'd set out to find my "self" in Idaho:
I found frostbite and little more.

So poetically I set her out there, not knowing more
than my mother knows. I fixed it so she couldn't say,
    "Dollars
are what I'm after, mister." I let her wander in Idaho
until a car, a silver car, stopped to find her gathering
her belongings, and smiling just this once,
for effect, in their car drinking their brandy in January.

Well, January's over, witch. Will this month bring more
once-in-a-lifetime poems to earn me dollars?
The witch said, "Go gather new wood in Idaho."

Boats, Say, with Blue Silk Sails

So one fine day, and with a bright boot of sun, say you leave
your wanderings and I mine, from one door you come
with your feet in a state of nevermind out across the yard
and the sun so hard. Say you come upon me
and I'm a stone or tree or bird's song and when we meet
there is a silence all about, the shouting sort,
and say you turn or tilt your head a bit or bend
to touch the stone or lift to reach the leaf, and say you've
left the food in pans there on the stove, the burners on,
the water running in the tub, the iron face down on the
    collar
of your favorite shirt, and while you're in your tilt with me,
and I could be a single feather, one particle of dust,
say the house behind you burns all down and floods and
    floats away
and you begin to notice what has just occurred;
you start to make a meaning about love and this and that
and things we wish would last forever, the list grows on
and holds these twigs and bones and bits of moon
until your hands become a thing you cannot get your mind
    around,
boats, say, with blue silk sails and a place to go toward
and you stand in the yard crying and you wave and wave
and finally you get to go away.

Lament

There came a time when Dante didn't matter,
when blue was just another Picasso marvel
and "throat" a word for shattered
dreams caught in someone else's novel
idea of how the world should run
along after its sleeping self, a rush
of idle men trying to have some fun
with all the women who would push
grocery carts through mindless markets,
women intent on coupons and sudsless laundry soap,
saving a dollar for ice cream later at the park
with the children who would rather elope
with blue-throated birds and dream
of hot chocolate, the kind with marshmallow cream.

The Fan

Five feathers from five birds are arranged
to resemble a fan. The fan is oriental.
The pattern these feathers reveal is not
what makes me crazy. I can see and love
the woman who wears a blue skirt
as she walks toward a tree. The tree
is not much taller than she.
And I can love the landscape.

I can even name four of the birds
these feathers came from. It's not knowing
the name of the fifth bird that makes me feel
as if I've awakened again from that old dream
of sunken bathtubs. It's the bird I can't name
that makes love a possibility after years of never-agains,
those times when the names of birds were only crow
and crow.

Pheasant, robin, cardinal, meadowlark, me.

The Lemons

We had to have new rinds come spring
for what the birds had left us with
was a joke we'd keep to tell each other
later, later, when winter came again
and the juice was gone, like it goes
in winter, with those hoof beats
we fear, those pounding ones, at night
when all the seeds have been spit out
to freeze. I told myself not to spit
like that. I told myself I'd catch it,
just like last year, when the horses
came and killed.

South for the Winter

I tell my son I don't know
why Tang went into outer space.
I tell him, while watching Donahue,
that a surrogate sex partner
is a surrogate sex partner.
Then my son talks about explosives,
about how we could take out part
of the living room wall, which is white,
and replace it with white explosives,
and when it blows up it would all be white,
and no one would be able to tell
that we just blew up our living room.
This is my son who is twelve,
who took apart his computer to find its brain
and who worries about his seventh-hour swimming class
because by then six other classes have peed in the pool.
This is my son who can cook his favorite foods.

When I was his age, I waited to be sixteen,
waited like a golden hawk circling, circling.
When twenty came, I wondered where the hawk wintered,
where the birds went to. I knew *south*, but that was not
    enough.
Now forty, I want the names of towns, the maps
of backyards, some photographs of a bird-like
southern comfort to hang on these white walls
so that when we blow them up,
feathers will be everywhere.

Speech

I was thirty years into learning
"sit down, shut up"
when, to get a degree
from a place of higher
ha-ha,
they tell me:
"You will take speech."
I take
"speech,"
and just begin to learn
"stand up, speak out"
when my grade turns up a grand
65.
I think that means
sit down, shut up.

Golden

I hear her sing O them golden slippers,
only she sings it slow,
taking ten seconds
on the first half of golden,
lingering the melody
to suit her mood,
then she sings those four words again,
this time saying golden
about fifteen times,
up the scale, down, shouts it,
whispers it like the night hard love,
breaks it down until it sounds
like Gregorian chants, then marching,
and next the Vienna Choir Boys
are living in her throat,
and all the while
she's elbow-deep in bread dough,
flour falling snowlike when
she tosses a handful in the air
on a fast golden,
and she looks up laughing
while all the skin of her neck goes smooth as notes,
and her not knowing I'm here watching.

—For my mother who, fearing cameras, left no photographs.

Gifts

I'd talk to them now,
bring warm drinks,
light the fire,
put on Vaughn Monroe's
"Racing with the Moon."

I'd say
this is where I live,
these are the trees
I see every morning,
this is the chair
where I sit while the sun
goes down,

this is the floor by my bed
where I kneel at night,
these are my slippers,
and this is the book I love the most.

I'd sing for my mother—
she always liked that;
and for my father
I'd never get old or fat.

I'd say, "Here, Daddy.
You put the angel on top of the tree."

Aunt Macy's Dream

Aunt Macy had a dream but never told it except
for certain little parts she would remember
on rainy days or when a "blue norther,"
as her mother called these storms,
would threaten to plow out the trees,
set them roots up
in the middle of Main Street.

She'd get a look about her eyes
(don't knock, nobody's home),
or forget to take her hands up from her lap,
and we'd know she was remembering the dream,
or dreaming. We'd ask her, but she'd only sigh.
Sometimes not even that.

One day, the wind blew
trash and leaves from the other side of town.
She sat in the same chair, hands in her lap,
eyes gone to China, but then she smiled,
or maybe it wasn't a smile, a point we argued
later as we told the story over and over
about how she said, "I can tell you now,"
changed around the mouth, and died.

Maybe Someday

Good hand, held blue here
from the freezing
from the fall
the way they found you.
Your hair's not right.
Even your mother says,
"His hair's not right."
I wet a comb.
How still you
How hold you
How cotton your hold
How heart your still
How this cotton fills
three years later.

Argument for More Sleep

It happens like this: one morning you don't get up.
This is followed by the desire to have a bell
at your bedside to ring for someone
who is waiting in the next room,
a person of great charm and wit
who will bring you things on a tray.

Let's say this person is a man, let's say the tray
is made of neon lights designed to fix up
your life with some electric wit.
Let's say you start to laugh, let's say the bell
explodes as you reach for it. Let's make the room
a balloon and have the man be someone

from your past, a fugitive with guns, someone
much more desperate than you, a man with a tray
that holds your favorite hats, reflecting a room
where you keep porpoises, a room filled up
with a million silent mouths, where the sound of one bell
would leave humanity groping for its pants and wit.

No. All this is wrong. Let's have just ordinary wit.
A common sentence fragment. An implied design. Someone
like me. A plain sound. A very simple bell.
Plain tea, one muffin, one pat of butter, a wooden tray.

A ghost to come in. A ghost to say, "Get up."
A leaking roof. A gust of wind. A haunted room.

I'm sick of this. Let's have it be the dying room.
Make those gerunds work some wit.
Let's get organized now so we can get up
and get our shoes on like a normal someone,
and let's dispense with the calla lily tray
and the idea, the whole symbol, of the bell.

O.K. Good job. There is no ringing bell.
We're dead now. No stupid little room
to lounge around in, no one in the wings, no tray
will be delivered, no red rose, no words to make wit
necessary. There's no nothing and no someone.
This is it forever and give it up.

God. If I don't get up, someone may
come into this room ringing bells,
carrying my name on a silver tray: "Twit."

My Main Muzo

is a black cat
who came for food
as I typed

and with her paw
made this poem:

./

and although this
is merely a re-creation
of her paw poem,

I offer it to her
so that she is hereby
immortalized

which interests her
as much as
when I showed her
a photograph
of my grandmother
Zenoma.

Nirvana or What Happens When You Think God Looks Just Like You

A skunk is walking home,
his white stripe like the middle line.
He thinks he's going
across the back of God

when a blue Chevrolet
brings the news:

everything
is something else.

Princess

Princess of the Wait,
you butter your muffins
with a diamond knife.
Animals nip your feet,
you pet them,
but they want meat.

Princess,
you change channels,
cook fish on a spit,
and notice that it's late.

You may be hungry,
but the King eats first
the banquet you have fashioned him
from bits of air and fresh, clean snake.

Send Me a Soldier

I

This is my student leaning in,
and no Athenian could have carved him better.
I've watched him run from the library
through a mist of rain; I've watched him
stomp his feet in the corridor, and I've seen
the color come up into his face,
his wet and shining face.

II

This is me imagining us
as we tip-toe over the bodies of our friends
right here in America at 7th and Broadway,
and this is the same place where we talked one night
about how to free the singing in our paper hearts,
and here is where it is dark now, as we gather the silence
and pretend to be stones, earnest in direction—
after all, where can stones go on their own—
and pretending to be solid, and pretending what else?

III

This is two voices addressing each other
over a heady and howling north November wind:
Can you get me into heaven on a vote? How?
By what you need my friend, and what you need,
what everyone needs, what every home in the world needs,
yes, my friend, what we need is angels.

IV

This is the stanza to be read in a clinically detached tone
to combat the subjective and make my language a foreign
    one:
Into it hurt wings and thorns thrown blankly,
so grieved over the death of whom I think and write,
so grieved that no elegy can help, no bell, no group
of laughing children, no requiem for the masses, nothing.
So, into it, into the hold of it all, I throw these things,
rejoicing in odd feathers and some red.

V

These are the lovers:
Tell me, she whispered, turning her head sideways
into where his words could reach her easier,
where she could feel his breath.
Tell me something I already know. Read my mind.
Tie me up. Tell me how a week ago I came to you all crazy.
Tell me rock of ages.

VI

I'm the maniac in the mirror now,
turning to admire my sons and daughters,
my lovers and the flag.
I'm the lady in the grocery store
with blue hair who nips your heels
with a grocery cart full of cat food and cottage cheese.
I'm the cheerleader with the scissor legs.

I'm six years old and missing my two front teeth.
I'm two and talking.
One and walking.
I was never born.

VII
It's November and the winds begin
long before we ever feel them.
I am the woman anonymous
who writes the hours of nevermind
in the room upstairs with no door.
I am the one who knows
how grand it is to say
never again on earth:
send me a soldier,
send me a soldier.

Send me a soldier.

Over the Acorn

One's a hooker, honest as October light gleaning through
    leaves.
I saw her without her trade secrets sitting small
and cross-legged and clean, saw her open a small book and
    weep.

One stole from me, stole my lover, my clothes, my precious
    oils,
stole my forever breaking heart, even stole the color of my
    hair,
and left me hanging, my head through the noose of nothing.
This was the one who sent the book the hooker wept for.

There have been many others, women of all shapes of mind,
and in each one of them, without a solitary slip,
was the palmistry of a transient God.

If women bear some odd responsibility for the keeping,
then there are certain apologies to say—
not over loudspeakers by two lunatics
driving a van through downtown World—

but more from the eyes of one animal to another,
like two squirrels over one acorn, who, just as they are
    ready
to fight it out for good, are struck by a desire to wink
and give this acorn to the final ground.

> —for Shine and Marla, thieves, goddesses.

He Speaks While She's
Hiding Her Stretch Marks

While I was over there,
I read and took long walks.
On weekends, I'd rent a cabin
at the beach where I'd go alone
and practice making soups
from vegetables and rice.
For company, I watched the sea,
admiring the way the waves
moved small things
and changed what was large.
One day a piece of knotted wood
washed nearly up to me.
I took it home and have it still.

What marks you
you've earned.
Let me see you
here

in the light.

Razzmatazz

Razzmatazz is what happens
when one soul touches another,
when you feel like you're in a strange house
and it's dark and you don't know where the light switches
   are
so you go feeling the bathroom wall,
sort of scared and sort of silly,
feeling around in the dark
feeling around in the dark
and then finding it.

Mr. Boggs, he came smack
into my life like a love note I forgot I wrote,
he came saunter saunter into my life,
and he said, "Hey," like he knew something,
like he had the goods on my family,
and he commenced to hang around.
I took a look at him, real hard,
like I was looking into his head,
like I was seeing what was there,
what's always been there,
and what's always going to be there.
I look at him like I'm a woman
who's been somewhere with one hand on her hip,
like a woman who knows better than to hang around
like he's hanging around me, and he said, "Hey,"
like I didn't hear the first time.
So I said, "I'll bet you sweat something awful
when you make love."
This is how the first talk ends.

Mr. Boggs comes oozing in
like that first drink of gin
when it warmed all the outside out
and the inside in,
and I say, "Boggs? Is that you?"
And he says, "Hey."

Now he gets a new word and thinks he's smart.
He's wearing everybody out, and he says to me,
he says "silk" like he's hoping I've got some on somewhere
when there's none showing, he says and says "silk"
real pitiful, like he's hopeful I'm more than I am,
like he's wanting to whip me some
to make me tender up to him.
I think all this over, see, while I look him over,
up from his toes to his tip, real slow,
lingering a bit here and a bit there,
lingering. I'm looking so slow that he's beginning
to feel that silk next to him,
he's beginning to think he's got his fingers
on some lace at last,
he's looking dog sick in the face,
he's starting to fold,
he's gone.
I say, "Hey."

Razzmatazz is talking.
I say it's dark dark dark dark white
and he says it's light light light light black.
We're both saying gray.
This is talking razzmatazz.

One morning Boggs is gone.
I tell myself he's in town.
Only that night he doesn't come back.
And the next and next and next.
I get to screaming until I'm sick.
Then one day I'm getting up some flowers,
going to bring them in the house,
make the place look happy if there's flowers.
And down the road he comes.
Flowers leave my hands going everywhere
and I'm running. I don't know anything
but him,
don't know the months
or where he's been
or if there's been other women.
I just know it's him.
Boggs is back.
My whole heart is him.
He takes me up off the ground,
carries me inside where everything happens again.
Next day, he's gone.

Pine and mope, pine and mope.
One day I say enough.
I get gussied up, practice bringing my eyebrow up,
that one eyebrow, rising like the bustle of Victoria.
I'm out to proud fluff him,
and folks will say,
"She's got that wild damn hair that the wind tried to tame
and a sassyfrass mouth stuck out in a pout;

she's got a warm about her make you burn your hands off
if you go too far, and you'll go too far, and she sashays
around, clicking off the distance between nothing and
	nowhere
in her black spiked heels. You go ahead. Touch her.
Go ahead. Your mind will end up where the wind doesn't
	blow,
where no trees grow. Someday, maybe, she'll give you
a glance, then throw her head back and laugh.
Just when you had hopes that she would fade, here she'll be,
standing like she's not waiting anymore,
standing like it's her turn,
standing like she doesn't remember who you are.
You'll go to speak her name, and just as those memories
burn through of what you used to do with her,
something will catch her eye.
She'll look past you, up past the sky,
and she'll salute God.
This is how she'll say, 'Hello, everybody else.'
This is how she'll say goodbye to you."

Razzmatazz, oh baby, Razzmatazz.
Life isn't worth much without Razzmatazz.
I cry because I'm getting older,
then turn my head and kiss my shoulder,
Razz-a-ma
Razz-a-ma
Tazz.

They Go Jazz

They're going somewhere first they stop
buy two moon pies
one RC cola and throw
one moon pie out the open top
that's how the lady does it
always says to the clerk
two moon pies   honey   and an RC cola
and that clerk his eyes don't move
from her fancy
she says
we get to going eighty
I'll throw this moon pie out
let the wind take it to Chicago
then she laughs
thrump the counter
with both hands and say

chicken in the car
but the car can't go
chicken in the car
but the car can't go
chicken in the car
but the car can't go
and that's the way to spell
Chicago

and the clerk forgets
to get her money
just like every time
and her man waiting in the car

gets out
goes around to her side
opens the door
and she gives him a bump with her hip
and she moves into that car
so fast
that he gets to grab air
and she doesn't spill
one drop.

Small Play Called Get the Beat

"I got the rockin' pneumonia." — *Chuck Berry*

SAGE: On this day, there will be messages from the sky.
    You will be able to recognize them at once
    and call them by name.
    Names like circumferential differentiation.
    Like moronical perpetual palsies.
    (coughs)
PEASANTS: Do wa do wa do wa.
    Get down. (coughing)
SAGE: In the afternoon, you will tie a turban on you head.
    This will remind you of future lives,
    and you will be unable to think of anything but
      camels
    and the fleas that live on them.
    (wheezes some)
PEASANTS: Ram a lam a ding dong.
    I say get down. (wheezing)
SAGE: By the time night gets to you, you will have
      forgotten
    everything you ever knew. This pleases everyone.
    You will speak in lost languages. *National
      Geographic*
    will show up with cameras. You will strap on your
      guitars
    and sing don't ever, don't ever, don't ever, don't
      ever,
    but sometimes do it.
PEASANTS: Boogie on down, Sage.

    Exuent Sage, Peasants,
    coughing, wheezing, laughing,
    fever of a hundred and two.

Saint Peter to the Boring Poet

The message of your
laborious pontifications
did not fall on deaf ears.
Notice this crowd.
They're the ones
who went out of their chairs
backwards
while slapping their heads
and laughing
as you droned on.

I'm sorry, poet.
The job of God is filled.
I can, however,
let you go back to earth
as a one-liner.
You can walk up
to folks who are cooking
in their backyards.
You can tell them
their monkey is on fire.

Explain:

Dew where mushrooms serenely sit,
a small skunk's morning yawn,
and a neat hole on the opposite side
of a beaver's gaping chest.

Explain: Target Practice again
to that girl you left screaming
in the front seat
of your big
Ford
truck.

Hunting

I can see him now:
A hunting trip up north,
he stoops to split the warm belly
of a not-quite-dead-yet elk,
then turns,
        just like that,
and asks me,
        just like that,
to make pancakes on the Coleman.

Henry Samuel Chesser Tours His Farm

This old wind sock does its job
and the roosters, they do theirs.
The windmill works and the wife
makes good gravy—it's an art,
her gravy—makes the day start out right.
A man can forget what he's got to wade through

if the gravy's good, and I've been through
some bad cotton in my time, had some jobs
made my knuckles bleed, jobs I'd have quit outright
if it hadn't been for something driving from inside. There's
no telling where this life ends up. You start
with a craving. Pretty soon, you've got a wife.

I could have done worse, could have got a wife
who screams or paints her face or looks through
catalogues all day. Mine's a quiet one. But I start
kissing on her neck or ears, and she's got jobs
for me—the sink, the yard. Different with women—theirs
isn't need that wakes them up. It's complicated. Right

when I'm dying for it, she'll say something like: "Now get
   this right.
A man needs to learn his soul and glory. That's why he's
   got a wife."
Once she patted my head and said, "There, there,"
like I was her little pup. I got so mad I threw

the butter bowl against the wall and said: "A wife's job
is to damn well finish what her husband starts."

She cried when I took her dress up and that made me start
to bite. It was like having the sky pull me right
through God's eyes when she stopped fighting to say, "Your
    job
is to stop the ache," and she whispered it from inside,
    this wife,
this woman who had never given back. I was done for.
    Through.
We went there that day. And I mean There.

She loved me the way *I* knew. Women. I love all they are.
And the butter hung onto the wall. My mind starts
that day again when I see the butter spots come through
this new coat of paint. "We got it right,"
is what I said to her and she kissed my face. My Wife.
Now, when I'm not working this place, I do my job:

I think of ways to start the ache up in my wife—
tonight I'll wait to touch her right there.
And the windmill will creak through the dark. That's its job.

Hunker

It was Hunker taught me how to kill a catfish
with a hammer, how to peel the fur right off a peach,
how to take the breath from a woman, make her mine for
   life.
Said it wasn't the size I was that counted.
Said it was the count.
Told me to tell her that in twenty
I would come, that she should count out loud,
that a woman loves that sort of thing
and needs to have her mind on something
other than respect and said when she
starts saying numbers I should put myself
as hard in her as I could stand
and keep her hips up high and go in deeper
every number until she cried, *"I'm dying.
You are killing me,"* and not to stop no matter
what, to tell her *count,* and not to
come until the twenty came and hold her head
so she would know the pleasure in my face,
and kiss her. And he said the next day
I should say *twenty* to her in a public place.
Shout it to her in the grocery store. He said
it worked for him. I tried it, but I only
got to ten. The first time. She was loving me
forever when we got to nine.

Opinionated Love Poem

When your lover
has his face between your thighs
and drinks joy into you
and you love his face
and you love where his face is
and then he brings his face to yours,
anoints you woman with yourself,

When you like this
and say to yourself, "I like this,"
and say to him, "I like this,"

When you go through
whatever other bullshit
you go through to get to this,

When this man can touch you
as you do,

Then you can relax.

Those who deny you this are dogs.
Leave them to their chains, backyarded,
straining.

Mind as Mirror

A doctor told me he once had a patient—
a woman—
who was so out of touch with reality
that she could imagine herself
imagining herself
having sex.

My cuticles got interesting
as I pictured her
imagining herself
imagining herself,

and this went on.

Elemental Ode

Ode to seasons, time, infinity,
love, orgasms, redheads, deadheads, half-wits, dim lights,
ode to life, birth, death, in that order,
ode to parenthood, doghood, cathood, dogwood,
all the other hoods and woods,
ode to sybil leek, reincarnation, karma,
ode to paranoia, acrophobia,
and to pissing in the dark,
ode to the experience of this poem
which you are about to receive from thy bounty
through christ our giggle
that was the baby laughing at the table
Amen.

Leaving

It's done again.
While I thought perfect doves,
the room filled up with crows.

"The crows came, honey,"
I'll tell him later.
"The crows came singing Baptist hymns,
singing for spacious skies,
singing the blues, blues."

"She said it was the crows,"
he'll tell the cops.
His mind won't let him think
how they lifted me
on great black wings
straight back into
van Gogh's moaning mouth.

The coroner will write,
"Flew into the mouth
of a deceased painter."

Maybe I should leave a note.
Something simple.
Like salmon and onions
in the key of C.
A treble clef.
A symphony.

The unwritten part
of my head.
A thousand violins
missing their strings.
A trumpet full of clay.
A drum roll
down the side of a cliff
at dawn.

Anatomy of a Very Nervous Breakdown

You shout Ophelia's mad songs
in the produce department
of any grocery store. You are
nude.

And you do it,
and you do it,
and you do it,

and when they come for you—
and they will come for you—

you give them

your impression
of your impression
of you
doing you,

and you do it so well
you never want out.

Taking the Sky Away

Winner this year
of the Miss Ugly Pageant—ha—
what I was was beautiful,
with Tupperware.
I soldered all those wires making
turn signals for Jeeps.
I emptied the bedpans.
See me driving the van that takes
the sick ones home after therapy,
see me stripping,
working the snakes,
babysitting Beth and Peter Widen,
stealing Colonel Widen's cigarettes,
thinking thirty years later of the German
who shot him down, then left him everything in the will.
O, the diva complex. Romantic fatal magnolias.
I think I'm singing to the dying
these high holidays of the spirit.
My friend, she was too married.
White supremacy in the southern deb.
Scorpions, my bed legs in jars.
My father setting the house on fire
trying to burn out the owl
my mother feared, the whole sky hauled off
in the smoke of these lives.

A Fantasy Death Has Just Before Dawn

We'll all get into this old red truck
and go a mile or so into the woods
where thistle grows thick, and I,
Death says, will show you the blood of twigs,
the anchor of roots, the way these leaves
can kill even the strongest hearts.
Your brothers—you do have brothers, don't you?—
they will help fix the flat and the jack will fall
because your mother—you remember her—
is bouncing her first grandchild on her bony knees,
or should we make them fat for the story's sake?
And you—you—will watch yourself
win several prizes for spitting watermelon seeds
while your father paces and paces back at the house,
lights his next cigarette from the one before it
and knows his family is lost in a forest
where everything grows green, so green
that he faints and forgets what day it is,
what planet, year.

Wake

So, on the day of his memorial service,
people come to the house bringing stuffed clowns
because the widow collects them, likes having them
    around—

it takes her mind off the terrible mess
he left behind in his dark office

where the model airplanes hang down
from the ceiling above three miniature towns
he made from balsa wood during his bliss

which was self-induced by vodka martinis
that he always drank beginning at noon
every day of his adult life, even Sundays,

when he would go to the club after praying on his knees
for God to please get him out of this one, please undo

what he had done the night before always.

While Making a Pencil Sketch of Eggs With the Sun So Perfectly Burning

I take it like a trooper
the news that I control
so little of the world.

My first grandchild
sleeps and turns
in a perfect world
inside my tender
and unmarried daughter.

My youngest son
deals cocaine from the porch.

What we all
go for
is the white
blinding us
inside the shell,
the silence of perfection,
the curve of it.

I draw an egg, another.

Celebration of the Small

Who yawn magnificent zeroes
and sleep curled around
only the miracle of sleep,

Who dream of rooms
and of playing the piano
and of playing the piano well,

Who wake like water at its source
and eat an egg,

Who curve into day
knowing death, and cheerful.

The Vessel

The harbor of a mind is never safe,
and barnacles abound when the boat docks.
Oars splinter, paint peels, the cabin rots.
The rope that holds me finally frays,
and I, adrift and sail-less on an open sea,
await the pirates who will come aboard for gold
and in their furor find an empty me.

Windhorses

I said wolves when I meant loneliness,
said angels instead of graves,
made my windhorses out of mud
and laughed when they couldn't fly.
I glorified moonlight
because I couldn't say
my neighbor's children
scream at night.
I thought if I could get it right
about the moon's perfect cold stare
that the words would shake me loose,
stop a slaughter somewhere,
as if standing in front of a bullet
changes its course.

I said wolves when I meant loneliness.

Usual Day

making pies, but here's the flour on the floor
making roads I am with the broom handle
saying to the man who rings the bell
and only wants to sell some encyclopedias
cibola! cibola!
watching the fear come over him like a new skin

kissed them off to school
I sing the saga of the garage sale nightgown
put on my idiot grin
follow the salesman out the door
grab his arm and say
part of the history of my art
emerged from the mud
at Gettysburg

hold his arm and say
this this this
is how my life is
and he smiles his idiot grin
so I tell him about my marriage
while putting my hand down my throat
reaching for a belly laugh

a hangnail rips my heart

The Speed of Stone

I know a woman who in her house keeps stones.
She puts them into common bowls and sets them out
on tables, counters, even on the mantle are the bowls
and bowls of stones. There is no pretending not to notice.
There is no thinking knickknacks. And her house is kept
cold. She wears her clothes in layers, and a cap,
a woolen cap, and gloves. She goes about her day,
the doors open in November, the leaves coming in and cats.
And she is not old; she is young and slender, the most
beautiful woman I have ever known. She makes tea,
plays Vivaldi. The last time I was there, we talked
and our breath was visible. She said it's different
for the stones. They have no breath in what they speak.
She says before the speed of light was the speed of stone.
She says I am too fast to know the motion of the silence
of the stones, how they name everything, how they are
the knowing. When she said this, the wind pushed
more leaves through the open door. One of the cats
yawned.

Big Dipper

Here in the north, frost forms before verbs or vowels,
takes the breath and appetite;
sentences end up in Siberia.
It is so cold we go crazy, eat fur, die.

In the south, we are long and lying in the sun.
Our conversations sweat, but we drink those juleps
and say Daddy, Daddy, Daddy.

The east is where we make a reservation for our funerals,
thanking God someone else
will drive us through the Bronx.

Out west, that's how we say it, "out west,"
we weather well and tan ourselves;
we hang the hides and during the night
a lady comes to sew the sky while meanwhile
the little children marvel at the punchholes
from her needle and say ridiculous things like
Big Dipper.

Pale Plums

Try a planet that has no taste for poetry, so it goes on
for miles of middle-class boarding schools with no transitions
glimpses aloof to other people in apartments   who is he
tired of smiling of course at the disaster of purchases
envelopes not to be handled by children indirect
quotations   were he alive and not buried under
seven tons an estimate of sand and whatever else it is
to villagers who had a language and some thumbs
burial rituals thanking the seas   how to honor
any lesson like we are all faced with personifications
bits pieces everything more vivid at the end but

where are the children who take it in and dress it up
and feed it tea   pronouns a perfect analogy to Christ
no dialogue no description faster faster and the bars become
a poem a blur with a writer behind who is sympathetic to even
the cause of the informed, the educated, the thorn covered
beasts from other planets who take our daughters *and*
our sons, the darkness at the expense of someone, something,
everyone, everything, at the heart of referential insanity—
everything, understand, and a maniac at the helm
of a long convalescence, the family photo albums
locked in the trunk of a Ford LTD, the recording that says
I am never here right now.

Some third-rate humiliation, stuck and unable to grow up,
   cynical,
from now on if you're not ready and the world is changing,
you're as good as dead. Characterization or not. One large
   eye.
The title and guest and respect. O. In the name of zero,
and a sky the color of pale plums.

Where Dragons Be

I have built a holy temple in my head
and placed an olive branch there, and a dove
is on my tongue's tip so that my words
will have a ring of peace to them.

There have been those who've said,
"You cannot build a temple here.
You have no permit. Your wood is wet."
They are the ones I've tried to heal.

There have been mistakes. The lame
have died. The blind gone deaf.
The smooth-skinned babies given leprosy.
I don't pretend to get it right.

But I do pray. And as I'm driven
from this town, I'll point to a place
called my heart. I'll say,
"This is the edge of the world,

this is the immortal me."
Those who know the history of maps and flesh
will know I've pointed to the place
where dragons be.

I Give Me That

I take these periodic prayers to mean
such imminence is waiting on the tail
of every solitary amen, such imminence,
such wasteland, so many trials,
so many jurors, so many deaths by the neck
until hung.

I take these periodic tufts of breath to mean
pasque petals go to arabesque in less
than a glance, in less than a fraction
of a glance, in less than anything anyone
can measure.

I take these periodic lives I live to mean
temporary is more than
temporary.

I take these periodic prayers to mean
I want another chance.
I give me that.

Nothing Can Future

Nothing can future the beauty of a leaf
fallen, falling, attached yet to the tree
or further the splendor of a frequent sun
slipping through fog in the hallelujah here
or make the bird song any less or more
than it can be, which is salvation,
which is to say the hooves of animals,
the feet of man, all proper
in the solitude of each,
which is to mean one mind saying to another,
two bodies touching, the dreams of all,
and the leaning toward home.